SLAVE SHIP

SLAVE SHIP
The Story of the Henrietta Marie

GEORGE SULLIVAN

Illustrated with photographs

COBBLEHILL BOOKS Dutton New York

Illustration Credits

Library of Congress, 23; Mel Fisher Maritime Heritage Society, 11, 69, (Cheryl M. Clark, 30; Dylan Kibler, 53, 55, 59, 62, 63, 64 bottom, 65, 67, 68; Frank Weeks, 10); *The Miami Herald*, A. Enrique Valentin, 12; David Moore, 17, 28 top, 64 top, 66; © Bill Muir, 15; *National Geographic*, 46; New York Public Library, 18, 40; Pequot Library, Southport, Connecticut, 25; Schomburg Center for Research in Black Culture, 21, 28-29 bottom, 36; George Sullivan, *ii*, 49, 54, 61, 71, 74, 75, 76; Wendy Tucker, 31, 48, 50, 57. Maps by Claudia Carlson, 34-35, 43.

Library of Congress Cataloging-in-Publication Data
Sullivan, George, date
Slave ship : the story of the Henrietta Marie / George Sullivan.
p.   cm.
Includes bibliographical references and index.
ISBN 0-525-65174-8
1. Key West Region (Fla.)—Antiquities—Juvenile literature. 2. Henrietta Marie (Ship)—Juvenile literature. 3. Slave trade—Juvenile literature. 4. Afro-Americans—Florida—Key West Region—Antiquities—Juvenile literature.   I. Title.
F319.K4S85   1994
975.9'41—dc20   93-47653   CIP   AC

Published in the United States by Cobblehill Books, an affiliate of Dutton Children's Books, a division of Penguin Books USA Inc., 375 Hudson Street, New York, New York 10014

Printed in the United States of America
First Edition 10 9 8 7 6 5 4 3 2 1

Acknowledgments

This book would not have been possible without the support and cooperation of the Mel Fisher Maritime Heritage Society and many of its directors and staff members. These individuals include Mel Fisher, President; Dolores Fisher, Secretary; Madeleine Burnside, Executive Director; David Moore, Maritime Historian and Principal Archaeologist of *Henrietta Marie* field operations; Corey Malcom, Director of Archaeology; Wayne Lusardi, Conservator and Project Advisor; and photographer Dylan Kibler.

Special thanks are due the National Association of Black Scuba Divers, and, in particular, A. José Jones, President; Oswald Sykes, who headed the organization's *Henrietta Marie* Project Committee; and Marion Sykes. Special thanks are also due Carla Williams of the Schomburg Center for Research in Black Culture, New York Public Library; the Prints and Photographs Division, Library of Congress; Carole Heinlein, President, Key West Maritime Historical Society; Mary Freedman and Meg McCreery, Pequot Library, Southport, Connecticut; Thomas Hambright, Monroe County Hill Russell Library; Francesca Kurti, TLC Labs; Bill Muir, Wendy Tucker, Carol Shaughnessy, and Claudia Carlson.

Contents

1
A Painful Link

At the Mel Fisher Maritime Heritage Society in Key West, Florida, on the third floor of an old building that serves as a museum and archaeological laboratory, there's a room where visitors can see relics from the slave ship *Henrietta Marie*, which struck a coral reef and sank in the Gulf of Mexico nearly 300 years ago. They are grim reminders of the slave trade and its horrors.

A steel cabinet contains dozens of pairs of shackles of different sizes, blackened iron loops that were used to secure the ankles of the human cargo. A stout metal bar closes the loops and is locked in place by a metal wedge. The shackles are clear evidence of slavery's terrible cruelties.

There are boxes containing thousands of tiny blue and yellow glass beads, and shelves of pewter bottles and tankards, which were meant to be traded in West Africa for human lives.

In tubs containing a special chemical bath, there are several decayed elephant tusks. Acquired in Africa and valuable as ivory, the tusks were being taken back to England to be sold.

The Atlantic slave trade flourished for more than three centuries, and thousands of slave ships were involved. No more than a handful of other

One of the dozens of pairs of shackles found at the Henrietta Marie *site.*

slave ships have been found in American waters. The *Henrietta Marie* is the only one that has been scientifically studied.

The remains of the ship were discovered in 1972, and recovery of the artifacts followed. In 1973, 1983, 1984–85, and 1991, thousands of artifacts were recovered, identified, cataloged, and restored under the supervision of marine archaeologists.

Today, for a small admission charge, a visitor can enter the Mel Fisher Maritime Heritage Society, a nonprofit educational and scientific organization that dates to 1982, and see many of the artifacts. An exhibit of *Henrietta Marie* shackles, trade goods, muskets and lead shot, hull and deck timbers, and other items is scheduled to travel to cultural institutions in New York City, Chicago, and other major cities.

Late in 1992, members of the National Association of Black Scuba Divers made their first visit to the museum. To these men and women, the artifacts were an awesome sight.

"Looking at the artifacts is much different than looking at photos in a book or even replicas of the artifacts," said Oswald Sykes, a retired mental health administrator and a member of NABS. "You react differently.

Divers and marine archaeologists began recovering artifacts from the Henrietta Marie *in 1972.*

Marion and Oswald Sykes examine a pair of shackles from the sunken slave ship Henrietta Marie.

"You cannot look at them without feeling real people were involved. And it's not just other people. It's *your* folks.

"Most of the tears come when you look at the small shackles. They look too small for even a woman's ankles. Those shackles were for a child."

Sykes's wife, Marion, calls the shackles, beads, and other objects in the brightly lit glass cases "a link to our heritage." She says, "Those artifacts hit home. Anybody black who sees them, tears start to flow. Just talking about them, my eyes start getting a little watery.

"They give you a feeling of pride. They mean, 'I came from somewhere, too; I've got a heritage, too.' "

In 1993, a dozen members of the National Association of Black Scuba Divers placed a memorial at the site where the *Henrietta Marie* sank. A bronze plaque fixed to the memorial pays tribute to the many millions of black Africans who survived the transatlantic crossing and the institution of slavery itself.

To date, there are few if any monuments in the United States dedicated to the African men, women, and children who were wrenched from their homes to be enslaved in the New World. The *Henrietta Marie* now serves as one such memorial.

2
Final Voyage

When the *Henrietta Marie* went down after striking New Ground Reef about 35 miles west of the island city of Key West at the southern tip of what is now the state of Florida, the vessel was on the last "leg" of its three-stage voyage. It had already off-loaded its cargo of perhaps as many as 400 slaves at Kingston, Jamaica, in the West Indies, the slave-trading capital of the Caribbean at the time. The ship was heading back to England.

Leaving Jamaica for the return voyage home, the *Henrietta Marie* sailed west. After rounding the western tip of Cuba, the captain planned to head east toward the Dry Tortugas, a cluster of small islands and coral reefs at a point near where the Gulf Stream meets the Atlantic Ocean.

But the *Henrietta Marie* never reached the Gulf Stream. Its voyage ended on the jagged coral of New Ground Reef, where the vessel broke in half. Part of the ship settled to the bottom behind the reef to become buried in sand. Ocean currents scattered the rest across the top of the reef to the south. All aboard went down with the ship.

The 120-ton *Henrietta Marie* was a typical merchant vessel of its time, three-masted, square-rigged, square-sterned, and some 60 feet in length. The ship was manned by a crew of 19 or 20 and carried eight cannons.

It is believed the vessel was named for Henrietta Maria, the French wife

Three-masted Henrietta Marie *was square-sailed, square-sterned vessel, and weighed about 120 tons.*

of English King Charles I. (The state of Maryland also takes its name from Queen Henrietta Maria.) Its French name and the fact that the ship is known to have been foreign-built suggests that the *Henrietta Marie* was French in origin.

Marine archaeologist David Moore, who has devoted almost a decade of study to the *Henrietta Marie*, says it was probably one of the 1200 or so vessels captured by the English during the war between England and France—King William's War—that ended in 1697. There are no known records concerning the operations of the *Henrietta Marie* before that date.

That same year, 1697, English military authorities are thought to have sold the *Henrietta Marie* to the highest bidder. Captained by William Deacon, the *Henrietta Marie* may have made its first voyage as a slave ship late in 1697. The vessel went first to West Africa and there traded for black Africans. The slaves were delivered in Barbados in 1698.

In 1699, the *Henrietta Marie* set out again, following the same triangular route. Thomas Chamberlain was now the captain. The ship went first to West Africa, next made port at Barbados for water and provisions, and continued to the island of Jamaica where the human cargo was sold. In July, 1700, completing the final leg of its voyage, the *Henrietta Marie* returned to London.

The ship's archaeological remains plus historical records found in London are evidence that the *Henrietta Marie* made at least one additional voyage. That was its fatal voyage, the one that ended sometime between October, 1701, and March, 1702, when the *Henrietta Marie*, undoubtedly off course and lashed by a violent storm, plowed into New Ground Reef.

At the time the *Henrietta Marie* left London in late 1700, heavily laden with trade goods and bound for the West African coast, black slavery was well established in the Caribbean, where the first efforts had been made to develop an agricultural economy in the New World. Europeans had come to realize that there were enormous profits to be made on such export crops as sugar, coffee, tobacco, cotton, and rice. The profits, of course, depended on cheap labor and plenty of it.

When the Spanish established their colonies in the Caribbean, they intended to use the local population—people they called Indians—to do the hard work. But the plan failed. The Indian population proved unwilling or unable to work as the Europeans demanded. Because of mistreatment

When the Henrietta Marie *struck the reef, the vessel broke apart. Hull timbers are barely visible on the ocean bottom.*

African slaves toiled on the West Indian sugar plantations.

and the rapid spread of such diseases as smallpox and typhus, the native Indians died by the thousands or ran away.

Slavery was the European solution to the problem. Only a few years before Columbus's first voyage to the New World, Europeans had discovered the West Coast of Africa. In the lands that framed the Gulf of Guinea, they found many places teeming with people. During the 1400s, Portuguese traders started seizing blacks who lived along the coast. They shipped these Africans back to Europe as slaves. They also forced blacks they captured into slave labor on sugar plantations they established on islands off the African coast that they had colonized.

During the 1500s and 1600s, as colonization expanded in the New World, the demand for African slaves grew by leaps and bounds. At the time of the *Henrietta Marie*'s last voyage, slave vessels were making regular visits to Caribbean ports. African slaves were in great demand to work on the sugar plantations.

No one knows for certain how many Africans were taken captive to be enslaved in the Americas. Estimates range from 10 to 12 million, although some historians say the figure could have been as high as 20 million. It has also been estimated that as many as a third of the Africans never completed the trip. They died from sickness, disease, or outright cruelty. One historian, recalling the enormous loss of life that occurred during the voyages, speculated that if the sea could be drained between the West Indies and Africa's West Coast, the paths of ships could be traced by the bones of Africans who died during the ocean crossings.

3
The Atlantic Slave Trade

 Of the millions of Africans sold in the colonies of the Americas, about 65 percent went to Brazil, Cuba, Jamaica, and Hispaniola, with most of the remainder going to British, French, Dutch, and Danish colonies. About 6 percent of all slaves were delivered to North America.

Often when Europeans sought to attack and capture African blacks, they fought back or took shelter far inland. Then the Europeans discovered there were Africans who saw nothing wrong with selling other Africans as slaves. Often these were tribal chiefs who were willing to deal in captives of defeated tribes, trading them for guns, cloth, glass beads, and a variety of other items.

African blacks who were sold into slavery also included debtors or those convicted of theft, murder, or other crimes. And during periods of famine, families sometimes sold off a family member. But Jamaica-born Colin Palmer, a professor of history at the University of North Carolina, says that as many as 80 percent of all slaves were captives taken in wars.

Nearly every nation in Europe was involved in the slave trade at one time or another. Portugal, France, England, and the Netherlands were among the first nations to undertake the delivery of black Africans to the Americas. The Spanish, although they purchased slaves in huge numbers,

Captured slaves were marched to forts on the West African coast which served as prisons. There they awaited the arrival of a slave ship.

did not become active as traders on the West African coast until the late 1700s.

England's interest in the slave trade escalated once they started to acquire colonies in the West Indies. The British began with St. Christopher and Barbados in 1624. They took control of Nevis in 1628, Montserrat in

1632, and Jamaica, destined to be the hub of slave trading activity in the New World, in 1655.

It was a natural step for the English to begin growing sugarcane in their newly acquired colonies. Barbados, a small island on the eastern fringe of the West Indies, where sugarcane cultivation was introduced in 1641, became known as the "mother of the West Indian sugar islands."

Jamaica, a good-sized island, larger than Puerto Rico, almost as big as the state of Connecticut, was also well suited for growing cane. Indeed, by 1700, Jamaica produced more sugar than any other nation in the world.

As part of their efforts to muscle-in on the trade in slaves, the English, in 1663, formed "The Company of Royal Adventurers Trading in Africa" to supply the West Indies with 3,000 slaves a year. Although the enterprise was headed by the brother of King Charles II, the Duke of York, it was not successful, suffering from poor organization and stiff competition from privately owned slave traders.

The private vessels—called "interlopers"—were so successful that Parliament passed legislation in 1698 that opened the slave trade to all. To be able to trade legally, however, private vessels had to pay a tax of 10 percent on the value of the cargoes they carried as they left for the African coast.

The *Henrietta Marie* is thought to have sailed as both an interloper and, after 1698, as a 10 percent ship. It is believed that the vessel was on its way from West Africa to Barbados when the Act of 1698 became law.

The West Indian plantations, where the sugarcane was grown and processed by primitive machinery, required huge armies of African laborers. Some West Indian islands resembled enormous prison camps where slaves toiled under brutal working conditions.

Black African slaves eventually came to outnumber whites on many islands. In Jamaica, as early as 1673, there were 10,000 blacks and 8,000 whites. By 1724, there were 32,000 blacks and 14,000 whites.

Whites became very fearful as a result. They enacted harsh laws that were intended to keep the enslaved blacks under control. The "Act to regulate the Negroes on the British Plantations" was passed in 1667. It referred to the African blacks as being "of wild, barbarous, and savage nature . . ." They had "to be controlled only with strict severity." If a slave struck "a Christian," he was to be severely whipped. If it happened a second time, he was to be branded on the face with a hot iron. If an owner accidentally whipped a slave to death, he was not subject to a fine or imprisonment.

Some slaves accepted the cruelties. Others sought to escape or rebel. In Jamaica, in 1673, 200 slaves revolted and killed twelve whites. There were slave uprisings in Haiti (Hispaniola) in 1679, 1691, and 1704.

During the late 1700s, antislavery voices began to be heard. In 1807,

An anti-slavery meeting on Boston Common in 1851.

the British Parliament passed a bill that outlawed the slave trade. The United States Congress banned the importation of African slaves in 1808.

England ended its participation in the slave trade in 1833 by freeing all the slaves in its colonies. The French abolished slavery in their colonies in 1848.

During the early 1800s, many of the Spanish colonies in Latin America won their independence. These new nations either immediately banned slavery or passed laws providing for the emancipation of all slaves.

In the United States, the deep divisions over slavery tore the nation apart, helping to trigger the Civil War. Abraham Lincoln's Emancipation Proclamation, which became effective on January 1, 1863, freed all the slaves in territories still at war with the Union, but slavery was not officially abolished in the United States until the ratification of the 13th Amendment to the Constitution on December 18, 1865. Cuba abolished slavery in 1886, and Brazil in 1888. Despite all the legislation, slavery lingers on in remote areas of Africa, Asia, and South America.

In the West Indies today, there are reminders of the slave trade and the sugar industry of centuries past—crumbling remnants of stone sugar mills and upended copper basins in which the juice squeezed from the cane was boiled and purified. But such relics aren't necessary to recall the infamous slave trade. As Colin Palmer has pointed out, Africa's children everywhere are the clearest evidence.

"African people in the New World were never truly vanquished," he says. "The fact that black people are still around means that they had to draw upon their inner resources, then and now, to survive as a people."

He adds, "Rather than bemoan the fact that the slave trade existed, that people underwent unspeakable kinds of things, the challenge now is not

The United States banned the importation of slaves in 1808, but the trade continued illegally. This engraving depicts the upper deck of the slave ship Wildfire, *captured by an American steamer and brought into Key West, Florida, in April, 1860.*

to forget all that, but simply to build upon that kind of past and go in positive directions.

"The slave trade was an awful thing. But people have to pick up the pieces and go beyond that."

4
A Slaving Voyage

Slave ship voyages were long and hard, often filled with suffering and despair for both the crew and cargo. They lasted a year or more.

The proper timing of a voyage was vital. A captain leaving Europe had to schedule his ship's departure so that the vessel would arrive at the West African coast with time to purchase slaves and still arrive in the West Indies when warehouses were filled with processed sugar or whatever goods he planned to take back to Europe. Weather, of course, was a factor that had to be considered.

As James Barbot of the *Albion Frigate* wrote: "I am of the opinion that the properest season to render the . . . voyages most prosperous and safe is to depart from Europe about the latter end of September to enjoy . . . the good season on the coast; and to have a sufficient time to carry on the trade there, so as to reach [the West Indies] by the latter end of April following, which is the time they make sugar there; that so ships may have their full lading, and sail thence for Europe before the season of the hurricanes there; and arrive here before the boisterous weather, which usually reigns on our coasts about the beginning of October."

The trip Barbot described required a voyage of thirteen months. A Royal African Company slave ship named the *Falcolnbergh* made eight voyages

This maker's mark for John Emes, Jr., which appeared on a pewter bottle recovered at the wreck site, helped to establish the Henrietta Marie's *departure date from London.*

between 1691 and 1704, with the average trip lasting fifteen or sixteen months.

The final and doomed voyage of the *Henrietta Marie* began in late 1700. Detective work by archaeologist David Moore proves this. One of the short and stubby pewter bottles found at the wreck site was found to bear a maker's mark that belonged to a London craftsman named John Emes, Jr. Moore learned that Emes was not given the right to use the mark until November 11, 1700. In order to be able to have one of Emes's bottles on

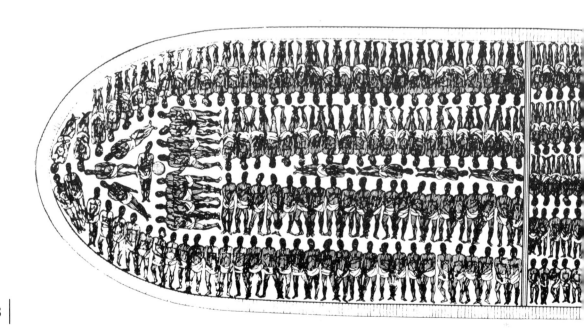

board, the *Henrietta Marie* would have had to have left London sometime after that date.

Upon leaving its London dock, the *Henrietta Marie* sailed down the Thames River and out into the Strait of Dover. There it may have anchored for a short time, waiting for favorable winds or perhaps the arrival of other slavers. As a protective measure, slave ships would sometimes sail in clusters to West Africa.

The *Henrietta Marie* was a typical merchant ship of the day, a type of vessel built long before shipbuilders began turning out vessels especially designed to carry slaves. Carpenters would have built platformlike shelves between the main deck and the hold, the lower interior space where food and water were stored. When loaded onto one of the platforms, a slave had space that measured 5½ feet in length, 16 inches wide, and 4 feet from top to bottom. He or she had to lie sideways; there was not enough room to lie flat.

Once the human cargo had been loaded aboard, the crew stretched

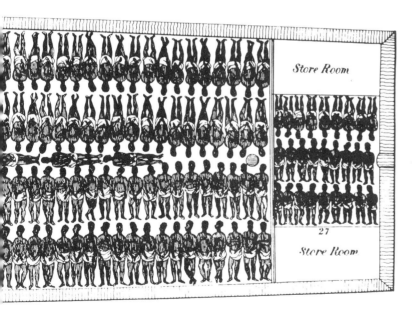

Abolitionists said the slave ship Brookes, *which was built to accommodate 451 persons, carried as many as 609 slaves on one voyage. This drawing from an abolitionist pamphlet published in 1839 shows the vessel's lower deck.*

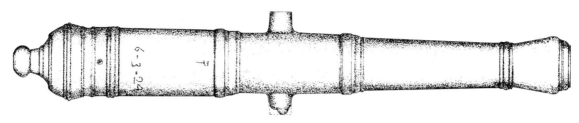

The Henrietta Marie *carried eight cannons of this type. Numbers on barrel refer to the cannon's weight, about 800 pounds.*

high netting along the side rails of the ship to prevent anyone from jumping over the side. In the afterpart of the vessel, they erected a heavy wooden barrier that separated the quarterdeck and captain's cabin from the rest of the ship. If the slaves rebelled and managed to get out of the hold and up onto the deck, the crew would barricade themselves in the stern where guns and ammunition were stored, until the uprising could be brought under control.

Like other merchant ships of the time, the *Henrietta Marie* was heavily armed—the ship carried eight cannons—and probably looked like a war-ship from a distance. From studying the ship's timbers, David Moore believes the *Henrietta Marie* was quite fast. Speed was a vital quality for slave ships. The owners looked upon the slaves as "perishable cargo." The longer the ship remained at sea during the Middle Passage—the voyage from West Africa to the West Indies—the higher the death rate got. Profits depended on delivering the slaves as quickly as possible.

Their speed made slave ships popular with pirates. Samuel Bellamy, a well-known pirate of the early 1700s, captured the English slaver *Whydah* early in 1717, and used it to plunder other vessels. The ship smashed up off Cape Cod, Massachusetts, late in 1717. Edward Teach, known as Black-beard, captured the French slave ship *Concorde*, which carried 40 guns,

| *A cannon recovered from the* Henrietta Marie *is delivered to a dock in Key West, Florida.*

and used it to prey on ships in the West Indies and in Atlantic coastal waters until the vessel went aground off North Carolina in 1718.

Ships the size of the 120-ton *Henrietta Marie* normally carried a crew of 19 or 20. Besides the captain, there was a first mate, second mate, a ship's boy to look after their quarters, a carpenter, cook, cooper, surgeon, and gunner. The boatswain was in charge of the rigging and sails. The deck crew worked for him.

Through wills found in London court records, members of the *Henrietta Marie*'s crew have become known. The earliest will is that of John Scorch, identified as a boatswain in the Royal Navy. It is likely he was boatswain aboard the *Henrietta Marie*. His will is dated October 18, 1697, just before the vessel left for Barbados, a voyage Scorch intended to make. From other records it is known that there was a Danish crew member. Peter Christopherson was a victim of the perilous Middle Passage. He died aboard the vessel on June 17, 1698.

Crew members of a slave ship often suffered the same infectious diseases that afflicted the black Africans. They also had to endure the brutalities of cruel captains. Some sources say the death toll for crew members was as high or higher than among the slaves.

The trip to West Africa could take two to three months, depending on the winds. The first land a ship from London sighted was likely the Cape Verde Islands, a group of Portuguese islands a little more than 300 miles off the coast of what is now the African nation of Senegal. Most slave ships stopped at Cape Verde to refill their water casks and replenish their food supply.

In general, the Africans who were brought to the Americas lived in the area between what is now Senegal and Angola, according to Colin Palmer. During the early 1700s, British traders frequently dealt with the Gold Coast, now the nation of Ghana, and perhaps that was the *Henrietta Marie*'s destination.

After their capture, slaves were brought to forts that served as prisons along the West African coast. Approximately fifty such forts were strung along the 300 miles of the Gold Coast's coastline. Well-known forts included Cape Coast Castle, Elmina Castle, Cormantine, Christiansborg. Gorée Island, now a short ferry ride from Dakar, Senegal, was also a holding place for slaves.

Within the forts, the captured slaves were kept in dark, damp, nearly airless dungeons until a ship arrived to receive them. Thousands of Africans are known to have died in these coastal prisons, victims of disease and injuries suffered during their capture.

At each fort, white slave traders called "factors" were stationed. The factor's job was to maintain friendly relations with the local Africans in order to be able to obtain captive blacks. When a slave ship arrived, the captain or his representative would negotiate with the factor, sometimes haggling for days.

Ships of the Royal African Company or other trading associations would usually remain at a fort until they obtained a cargo. But independent traders, like the *Henrietta Marie*, were not permitted to use established forts to obtain their slaves. They had to deal instead with independent agents or African traders directly. And instead of trading at just one place, three or four stops might be necessary. For some independent traders, it might take as long as six to nine months to acquire their cargo.

The price of slaves was governed by the law of supply and demand. When competition was high, prices rose. Prices also depended on the age and physical condition of each slave. Captive slaves were made to strip naked and each was carefully examined by the ship's captain. He felt their muscles and made them jump up and down. Shortness of breath meant rejection. Teeth were examined. Decaying teeth were taken as a sign of old age. Many more men were purchased than women. Every slave chosen was branded with the purchaser's mark on the shoulder, breast, or buttocks.

Arrangements for food and water for the Middle Passage had to be made. Traders realized that slaves were better able to endure the long voyage when they ate foods to which they were accustomed. In 1705, the

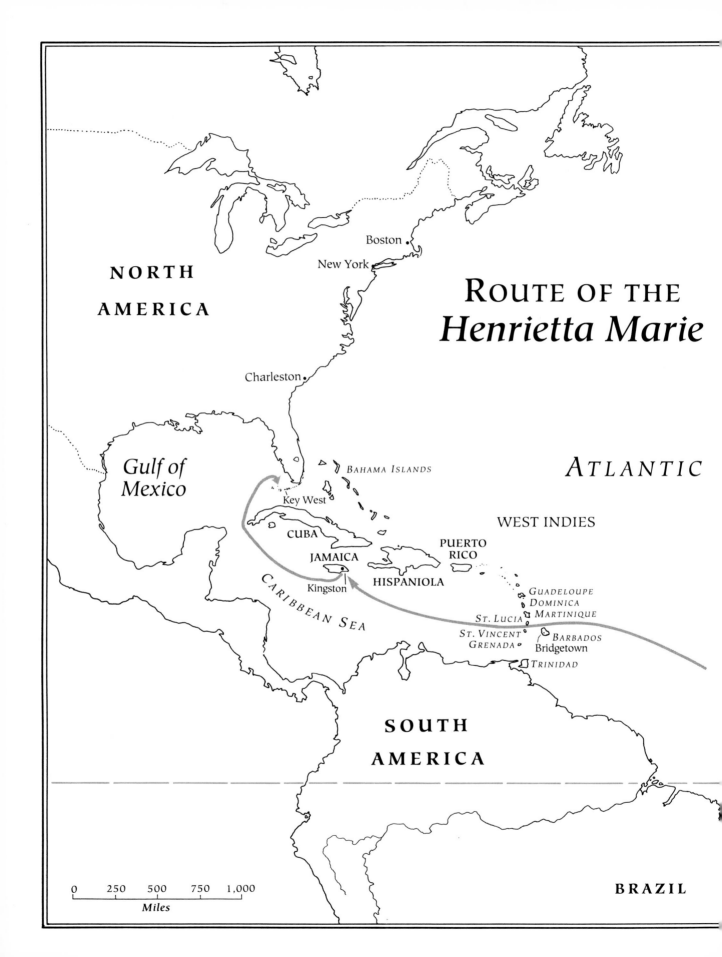

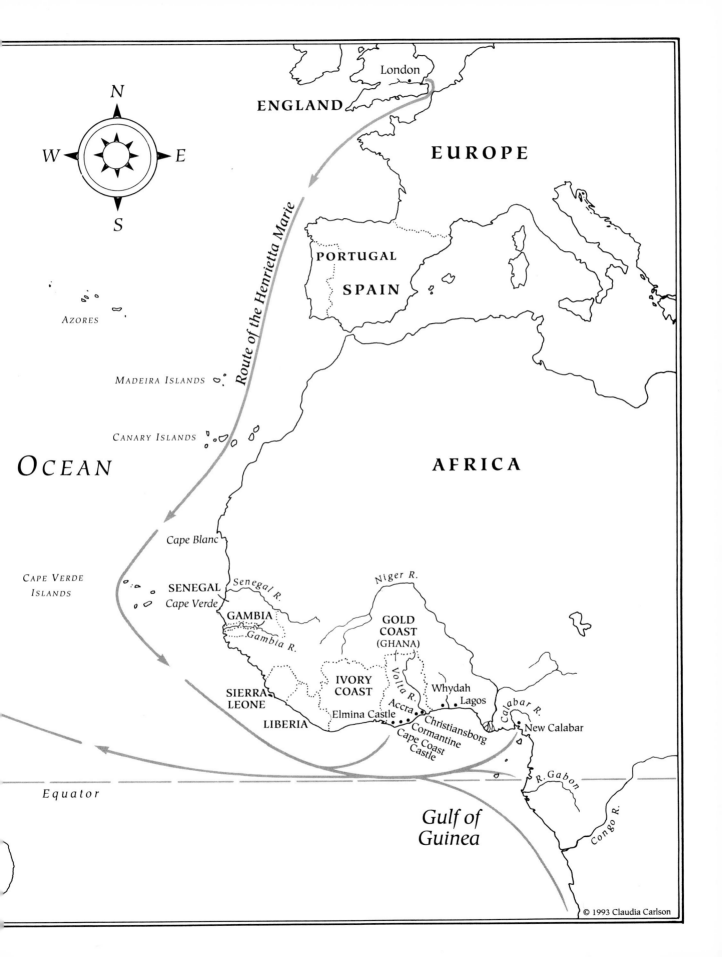

factors at the port of Whydah recommended corn, yams, malaguetta peppers, and palm oil for the captive blacks. All of these could be obtained from local traders. English slave ships also carried beans, bread, cheese, beef, and flour purchased in England.

Most black Africans fiercely resisted their capture, sale, and transportation to an unknown world. Purchased slaves were marched to the beach in chains under armed guard, then forced into long, round-bottomed canoes and rowed out to the ship. They would leap out of the boat or off the ship if given the slightest chance. They preferred death by drowning to being enslaved.

One can only imagine the confusion and terror African blacks must

Aboard ship, captured slaves were shackled and thrust into ship's hold.

have experienced in their first moments aboard a slave ship. One frightened young slave, Olaudah Equiano, captured in the interior of Nigeria about 1745 and put aboard an English vessel, survived the terrible ordeal to later write of his experiences.

Olaudah was only eleven years old when he and his younger sister were kidnapped from their home while the adults were working in nearby fields. He was made to join a long procession of chained men—called a "coffle"—and marched to the coast. Getting there took weeks of travel.

In his autobiography, Olaudah revealed how it felt to be taken aboard a slave ship. Fear was an overriding emotion, for he fully expected to be slain and eaten by his captors, whom he thought to be savages.

"Their complexions, differing so much from ours, their long hair and the language they spoke, which was different from any I had ever heard, united to confirm me in this belief . . . Quite overpowered with horror and anguish, I fell motionless on the deck and fainted. When I recovered a little, I found some black people about me . . . They talked to me in order to cheer me up, but all in vain."

Olaudah quickly realized that he had no chance of ever returning home, or even getting back to shore. He was led to a hatchway in the deck and ordered down into the dark, smelly cargo hold, already filled with slaves brought aboard earlier.

"There I received such a salutation in my nostrils as I had never experienced in my life. . . . I became so sick and low that I was not able to eat . . . I now wished for the last friend, Death, to relieve me."

Olaudah's captors made his situation even worse. "Soon, to my grief, two of the white men offered me eatables and on refusing to eat, one of them held me fast by the hands and laid me across the windlass and tied my feet while the other flogged me severely. . . . If I could have gotten over the nettings, I would have jumped over the side, but I could not. The crew used to watch very closely . . ."

Afterward, Olaudah met members of his own tribe among the captured slaves. They managed to relieve his distress somewhat. "I inquired what was to be done with us. They gave me to understand we were to be carried to these white people's country to work for them. I then was a little revived, and thought if it were no worse than working, my situation was not so desperate. But I still feared I should be put to death, the white people looked and acted in so savage a manner. I have never seen among my people such instances of brutal cruelty . . ."

But the worst was still to come.

5
One-way Passage

The voyage to the West Indies from the coast of West Africa—called the "Middle Passage"—piled one horror upon another. The more slaves a ship could carry, the greater the profit, so traders wedged as many bodies as possible into the cramped ships' holds. Shackles and whips were used to control the unruly.

For a vessel such as the *Henrietta Marie*, the crossing from West Africa to the West Indies took something more than forty days. With some 400 bodies packed closely together, the conditions belowdecks were hellish. The human cargoes were heaped onto wooden platforms. There was not space enough for an adult to stand erect or even lie down flat. Sickness and disease were rampant. The stench became unbearable. As the death toll mounted, it is said that sharks often trailed slave ships to feed on the bodies thrown overboard.

Slave uprisings were one of the greatest fears of the captain and crew. They knew they could expect no mercy from the slaves should they gain control of the ship. Any hint of rebellion brought harsh punishment.

The greatest threat of revolt occurred just after the ship had been loaded and before it left coastal waters, when slaves were still in sight of land and in good physical shape. Ships' crews often shackled the slaves in pairs,

Anti-slavery drawing of 1833 shows slaves thrown overboard during Atlantic crossing.

with the right ankle of one linked to the left ankle of another. The 80 sets of shackles recovered from the *Henrietta Marie* site are a reminder of this grisly practice.

Capt. Thomas Phillips of the slave ship *Hannibal* wrote in 1694, "When slaves are aboard we shackle the men two and two while we lie in port and in sight of their own country, for 'tis then they attempt to make their escape . . ."

On some vessels, slaves were taken up on deck from time to time for fresh air and exercise. At such times, the crew cleaned and disinfected the hold with vinegar, thought to be an antiseptic. Such attempts at sanitation did little to prevent the onset of smallpox, yellow fever, malaria, and other diseases.

Although its ultimate destination was Jamaica, it is likely that the *Hen-*

rietta Marie first stopped at the island of Barbados for fresh water and provisions. The captain may even have sold some slaves there. The island was well suited for growing sugarcane. Bridgetown, the largest city and the capital, was a busy slave port.

The ship that carried Olaudah Equiano had Barbados as its destination. He described the vessel's arrival there.

"As the vessel drew nearer, we plainly saw the harbor and other ships of different kinds and sizes and we soon anchored amongst them off Bridgetown. Many merchants and planters came on board . . . They put us in separate parcels and examined us attentively . . ."

Healthy slaves were usually brought ashore and sold at a "scramble." The buyers and the ship's captain would first agree on a price to be paid for each man, woman, or child. Then, at a signal, the buyers would rush among the terrified Africans, each trying to be the first to seize those he had chosen.

Olaudah told of the anguish caused when family members were separated from one another. "I remember in the vessel in which I was brought over . . . there were several brothers who, in the sale, were sold in different lots; and it was very moving on this occasion, to see and hear their cries in parting." Olaudah himself was sold in the Bahamas and later resold to a plantation owner in Virginia. He was purchased a third time by the captain of a visiting English ship, who took him to England. Later, the captain took him to sea as a servant, and eventually Olaudah won his freedom.

After taking on water and provisions in Barbados, the *Henrietta Marie* sailed for Jamaica, about 1,200 miles farther west. The trip took two or three weeks.

The British had seized Jamaica from the Spanish in 1655. It was a turbulent country. Slaves, who had escaped into the mountains when the British arrived, often terrorized plantation owners. Called Maroons, these Africans eventually managed to develop their own culture and live outside British control.

After delivering its slave cargo in Jamaica, the *Henrietta Marie* took on 81 hogsheads of sugar. The hogshead was a very large barrel or cask. Each held about 1,400 pounds of sugar. The captain also purchased or traded for bales of tobacco and cotton, and bundles of logwood, which provides a purplish dye for cotton and wool. Several two- and three-foot lengths of logwood were found at the *Henrietta Marie* site. "Those 81 hogsheads of sugar took up just about every inch of space in the *Henrietta Marie*'s hold," says marine architect Bill Muir, who has studied the ship's construction features. "You couldn't get another one in with a shoehorn."

Once loaded, the *Henrietta Marie* left Jamaica for the return voyage home. Upon clearing Kingston harbor, the ship headed west, the usual route, to take advantage of prevailing winds and currents. Vessels returning to England from Jamaica could also travel east, a voyage that took them through the Windward Passage at the eastern tip of Cuba, a shorter but more difficult route.

Historians and archaeologists believe the *Henrietta Marie* left for England some time before April, 1702. When England's King William III died early in 1702 and Queen Anne became the English ruler, war with France immediately broke out. One of the first things the French did was post a fleet of warships off the western end of Cuba to intercept English merchant vessels. The governor of Jamaica issued a warning to English ships in April, 1702, to avoid the waters off Cuba's western tip. Since the *Henrietta Marie* took the western route, the ship had to sail before the warning was issued, before April, 1702.

The voyage to the west took the *Henrietta Marie* around Cuba's Cape San Antonio. After rounding the Cape, the captain planned to sail north and east toward the Dry Tortugas, a group of small islands which lie about 45 miles west of Key West at the entrance to the Gulf of Mexico. There the vessel would pick up the Gulf Stream, the strong ocean current that flows north along the southeastern coast of the United States. Somewhere off the Carolinas, the vessel would turn east toward Europe and cross the Atlantic.

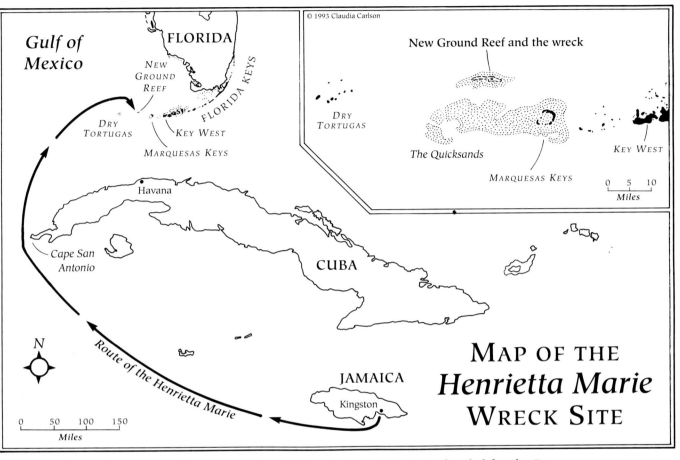

After sailing around the western tip of Cuba, the Henrietta Marie headed for the Dry Tortugas, but somehow got north and east of the islands and into the treacherous waters of New Ground Reef, its resting place today.

The Dry Tortugas were a "navigational hub" of the day, says David Moore. Navigation guidebooks gave signs that ships' captains were to look for as an indication they were approaching the islands. The sand at the ocean bottom, which navigators would sample, took on a particular color. Long, broad strands of eelgrass, which grows in shallow water, were another tip-off.

43

Somehow, the *Henrietta Marie* got too far north of the Dry Tortugas. David Moore speculates that the ship may have been the victim of a navigational error or perhaps it was blown off course by stiff winds. The *Henrietta Marie* wasn't the first ship to get lost and in trouble in these waters. A 1971 survey of shipwrecks in the immediate area of the Dry Tortugas conducted by the National Park Service pinpointed 195 wrecks.

Once he became aware of the error, the captain is likely to have reversed course and started making his way south, and the ship strayed into the waters of New Ground Reef. There the ledge of coral lurked, rising to within a few feet of the surface. The reef was unknown to navigators of the day. It was not marked on any chart.

Besides the reef, the *Henrietta Marie* had violent weather to contend with. David Moore believes the ship was pounded by a "norther," a type of storm that sweeps south off the Great Plains of the United States during the winter months and into the Gulf of Mexico. A norther can whip up with no warning. Heavy rains pelt down. Winds can reach 60 to 70 miles an hour, and the temperature plunge 10 to 15 degrees in fifteen minutes. Sailors of the late 1600s and early 1700s looked upon those ferocious storms as true hurricanes.

Lashed about by the storm and violent sea, the *Henrietta Marie* was helpless. A huge wave lifted the vessel and slammed it down onto the jagged coral. The ship broke in half. One section settled to the bottom to become buried in sand. Powerful currents scattered the rest across the top of the reef and beyond. Among the twenty or so crew members aboard, there were no known survivors.

6
Discovery of the Wreck

For almost three centuries, the *Henrietta Marie* lay undisturbed beneath the olive-green waters of New Ground Reef. In time, the remains of the ship became blanketed in a mix of sand, fine clay, and coral marine growth. So thick did the encrustations become that a diver could swim right over the ship's timbers and never even realize they were there.

The *Henrietta Marie* could not escape detection by modern technology, however. In the summer of 1972, Mel Fisher, the famous treasure-seeker, was searching the waters off Key West for the *Atocha*, a Spanish galleon laden with gold and silver that, along with several other vessels, had been wrecked in a hurricane in 1622. The hunt had been going on for four years.

Holly's Folly, commanded by Bob Holloway, was one of Fisher's search boats. A trim 34-foot Chris-Craft, *Holly's Folly* cruised a carefully laid-out pattern while towing a cylinder-shaped magnetometer, an electronic instrument with the ability to register fluctuations in the earth's magnetic field. It could thereby detect the presence of iron objects, such as ships' anchors or cannon. When the magnetometer registered a "strike," a buoy would be tossed overboard to mark the spot, and then a diver would go down to see what had been detected.

Mel Fisher's quest for the Spanish galleon Atocha, *laden with $200 million in treasure, led to the discovery of the* Henrietta Marie.

Aboard *Holly's Folly*, Holloway had an all-woman crew made up of his sister, Marjory Hargreaves, and Kay Finley. One August afternoon, *Holly's Folly* was plowing through the Gulf waters, the magnetometer trailing behind, with Holloway at the wheel. Suddenly Marjory Hargreaves, who was watching the meter that registered what the magnetometer was sensing, saw the needle swing sharply to the right. "Strike!" she cried out. Within seconds, Kay Finley took over the wheel and Holloway seized a buoy with its cement block weight and tossed it over the side. Back at the wheel, he made a couple of passes over the site to be certain the buoy was at the right spot.

Once he had anchored near the buoy and shut down the engines, Holloway put on a mask and flippers. The water was only about 17 feet deep and he was in a hurry, so he didn't bother strapping an air tank to his back but merely tucked one under his arm. He climbed over the boat's rail and into the water.

46

As Holloway made his way down toward the bottom, he looked for the buoy that marked the magnetometer contact. The summer sun flooded the world below with a dark green light. Holloway had no idea what the magnetometer had detected. He just knew it was something very big. On previous dives he had "discovered" such objects as a baby carriage and grocery carts, engine blocks and practice bombs left over from World War II.

Scanning the bottom, Holloway saw a long, heavy, cylinder-shaped object that was supported by a couple of feet of coral. It looked as if it were on a pedestal. Although it was covered with marine growth, Holloway knew that he had found an iron cannon.

Searching the area near the cannon, Holloway discovered a pair of metal rings connected with a metal bar. These were shackles. "There was no doubt they were leg irons," he recalls. "I had seen pictures of them."

Once back on board, Holloway radioed another of Fisher's boats, the *Virgilona*, and reported what he had found. A 46-foot wooden workboat, the *Virgilona* had several divers aboard and was equipped with air compressors and plenty of dive tanks. The *Virgilona* would do the salvage work. Holloway was eager to move on and resume his search for the Spanish treasure ship.

It didn't take long for the *Virgilona*'s divers to recover hundreds of artifacts. They brought up more iron shackles, an iron anchor, stacked pewter plates, metal tankards, an ivory tusk, a musket barrel, lead shot, fragments of a knife blade, and several spoons. Markings on the spoons helped to establish that the wreck was probably English.

No one knew the name of the ship at that time. But it had so many different kinds of things aboard, Holloway recalls, "Divers called it the H.M.S. *Woolworth*."

Fisher sent the *Virgilona* back to the wreck site in 1973 and more artifacts were recovered. By this time, he was convinced there was no gold or silver to be found amidst the shackles, glass beads, and pewter dishes his divers were bringing up, so he decided to move on and con-

A cannon from the Henrietta Marie *is encased in thick marine growth.*

Marine archaeologist David Moore began the recovery and study of Henrietta Marie *artifacts in 1983.*

centrate all his efforts on finding the *Atocha*. (It was 1985 before he did locate the *Atocha* with its precious cargo of gold, silver, jewelry, and emeralds worth an estimated $200 million.)

In 1983, a new team began work at the site of the English shipwreck. Headed by Henry Taylor, a specialist in underwater salvage, it included marine archaeologist David Moore. Moore had worked on several underwater archaeological projects. The *Henrietta Marie* and historical research concerning its artifacts would be an important part of his life for most of the next decade.

49

Moore returned to New Ground Reef in 1984 with Tony Kopp, aboard Kopp's 91-foot schooner *Illusion*, and spent several additional weeks there. The site was not visited again until 1991. In September of that year, Corey Malcom, head archaeologist for the Mel Fisher Maritime Heritage Society, led a team of divers to the wreck site to recover a cannon, which was to be used in an exhibition of artifacts recovered from the wreck.

Getting to the artifacts and structural remnants of any sunken ship is a difficult challenge. Divers and marine archaeologists call upon a wide range of equipment, everything from Ping-Pong paddles (which have been used to fan away deposits of loose sand) to highly computerized deep-diving robots and manned submersibles.

The water's depth at the *Henrietta Marie* site is not much of a problem. At the crest of New Ground Reef, the water is only 10 to 12 feet deep. As the reef slopes downward to the south, the water gets to be 30 to 40 feet in depth. At such depths, the bottom is reachable by divers wearing scuba gear. But one of the problems at New Ground Reef is a slack tide. "If there are no currents," says Corey Malcom, "a cloud of silt surrounds the area, and just goes nowhere. It's zero visibility. All work must be done by feel." Slack tide arrives every six hours.

The *Henrietta Marie* wreck site is typical in that the remains of the ship are cloaked in thick sand or sediment. Divers use small hand-held airlifts for removing loose sand and mud from the search area. Often powered by a compressor on the boat deck, these operate on somewhat the same principle as a home vacuum cleaner, sucking up debris wherever they are aimed.

Once the top layers of sand, mud, or loose coral have been removed, divers with hand-held detectors scan the area searching for anything made of metal. Recovered objects are brought to the archaeological laboratory where they are washed, sorted, numbered, and cataloged, then studied.

Marine archaeologist Corey Malcom examines a heavily encrusted metal artifact found at the Henrietta Marie *site.*

At the Henrietta Marie *site, the Gulf of Mexico is no more than 40 feet in depth, putting the ship's remains within easy reach of scuba-equipped divers.*

Most are either metallic, mineral, or organic. No matter what they're made of, almost all artifacts require special treatment.

Anything made of wood must be kept wet. Ship timbers, if allowed to dry out, would splinter into hundreds of tiny pieces. Iron objects that have been in salt water for long periods of time become corroded; they rust. They also become covered with a thick blanket of coral limestone, made up of the skeletons of tiny sea creatures. As a result of this encrusted material, recovered objects only slightly resemble their original form. A cannonball may look like an oddly shaped stone. A sword may have about the same shape as a loaf of French bread. Countless objects are so distorted nobody knows what they are.

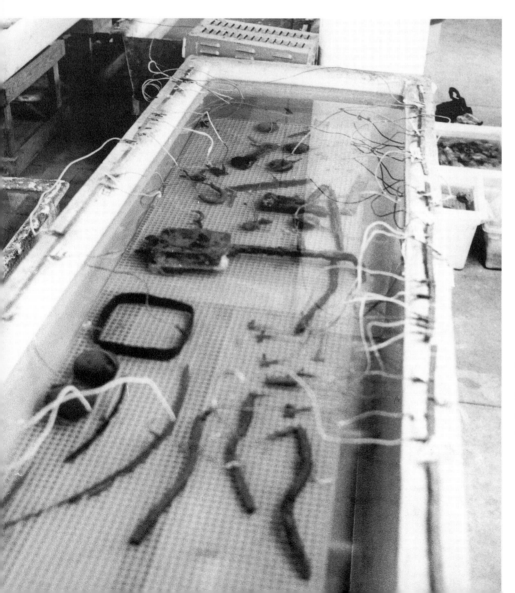

Metal artifacts from the Henrietta Marie *undergo restoration at the Mel Fisher Maritime Heritage Society in Key West.*

At the laboratory, the encrusted material is first chipped away from each artifact. Then the coating of rust has to be dealt with. Iron and some other metal objects are restored through electrolytic reduction, or electrolysis. The objects are placed in a plastic tank or tub containing a liquid chemical, usually caustic soda. A steel plate is suspended in the liquid at one end of the tank. Wires connect the various objects. Electric current is passed through the liquid, causing a chemical reaction. Small bubbles appear on the surface, a sign that chemical changes are taking place.

It doesn't happen overnight. It may take months to restore a small object, such as an iron spike. An iron cannon barrel may require a year or more of such treatment. Artifacts have to be washed occasionally during the process. When the treatment is completed and the objects have been allowed to dry, they are coated with an acrylic spray.

The artifacts recovered from the *Henrietta Marie* required several years of work on the part of laboratory workers and museum curators before they were ready to be displayed to the public. To marine archaeologists such as David Moore they make up a "rare collection" of physical evidence representing a wretched period in world history.

Coral limestone coats a 300-year-old metal drinking cup, or tankard.

7
What They Found

The archaeologists and divers working at New Ground Reef recovering artifacts always referred to the ship that sank there as "the English wreck." No one knew its name. Thanks to a startling discovery made in 1983, "the English wreck" stopped being a mystery.

That year Henry Taylor's salvage team, operating from the *Trident*, a 28-foot dive boat, began work at the site. Besides Taylor, the crew included David Moore, Jimmy Amoroso, and Duke Long. All four were expert divers.

Late one July morning, the *Trident* arrived at the site for a day of work. While Taylor and Moore were busy setting the anchors that would keep the *Trident* over the area where the divers were to work, Duke Long put on a dive mask and flippers and plunged into the water. "Duke had a habit of always jumping into the water first to see what the visibility was like," Moore recalls.

Moore and Taylor had finished deploying the anchors and were on their way back to the *Trident* when they saw Long in the water at the boat's side. "Hey!" Long shouted, "you're not going to believe this!"

Long had placed the object of his excitement on the *Trident*'s deck, where it rested in an expanding puddle of water. Although thickly encrusted with marine growth, it was obvious from its shape that it was a ship's bell.

The bell was 13 to 14 inches in height. About two-thirds of it was coated with marine growth. The other third had apparently been buried in sand and not exposed to the salt water. That part was smooth to the touch and had a deep green sheen, an indication the bell was bronze.

Moore could hardly control his excitement. A ship's bell was a very rare find. From a historical standpoint, it could have enormous value. He knew that a wealth of information could be derived from it.

Moore placed the bell on the carpet-covered housing over the *Trident*'s engine. The four men stood back and admired the find. Jimmy Amoroso

After marine growth was chipped away from bell's waist, ship's name was revealed.

said, "Maybe the thing's got a date." Moore replied, "You know, you could be right."

Moore then began to flick off some of the wet marine growth that surrounded the bell's waist with a fingernail. To speed things up, he got a screwdriver and began to gently pick away. Since the bell was bronze, the encrusted material merely coated the outer surface. Had it been iron, the marine growth would have bonded to the surface and removing it would have required special chemical treatment.

As the encrustations began to fall away, the upraised symbol of a letter or number began to appear. It was the number "9." Moore now realized he was working around the bell's waist in the "wrong" direction, that is, from left to right, and the "9" was probably the last number in a four-digit date. "Wow!" Moore cried out. "Here we go!" and he set to work again.

Within minutes a second "9" appeared, then a "6," and then a "1." The "English wreck" had a date—1699.

Moore and the others could hardly believe their eyes. They stared down at the bell and rubbed their fingers over the upraised numbers. Moore snapped some pictures.

"Hey!" said Jimmy Amoroso. "Maybe there's a name on there, too. You've got a lot of encrustations left."

Moore picked up the screwdriver again. Quickly, the letter "E" began to take shape. Then came an "I," and "R," and "A" and then "M." Moore gasped. The letters spelled out MARIE.

"We've got a name!" Moore shouted. "We've got a name!"

Amoroso was less excited. "Maybe it's got two names," he said, "like *Santa Maria.*"

"Maybe you're right," Moore said, and started to work again.

Sure enough, the letters forming a second name began to appear. When Moore had finished, they spelled out the name HENRIETTA. There were still some encrustations remaining. "Maybe she's got three names," David said with a grin. "I'll continue." Before long, the word THE became visible.

Pewter spoons recovered at the Henrietta Marie *site helped to establish the ship's English origins.*

Around the waist of the bell, the words now stood out clearly: THE HENRIETTA MARIE 1699.

"It blew me away," says David Moore.

The bell is thought to be a "watch" bell, used on naval vessels to sound every half hour and mark the "watches," the time periods crew members are assigned to duty.

The bronze bell with the name and date was a key that helped to unlock many secrets. Henry Taylor called on Peter Earle, a noted British historian and author, to search maritime records in England for information about a ship named *Henrietta Marie*. In newspapers of the late 1600s and early 1700s, in a section titled "Jamaica Shipping Returns," Earle found references to the *Henrietta Marie*'s sailing schedule. He also learned that the vessel was foreign-built, 120 tons in size, square-sterned, and carried eight guns.

The date 1699 on the bell would seem to indicate that the ship had made its first voyage that year. But historical research by David Moore revealed that the *Henrietta Marie* made at least one voyage at an earlier date. That fact led historians to believe that the ship's original bell had been replaced, perhaps at a time the vessel was being overhauled or refitted.

The bell, of course, was only one of many thousands of artifacts recovered at the *Henrietta Marie* site. Many were of pewter, a metal made of tin and lead. Before glassware came into general use, tableware and kitchen utensils were often made of pewter. Divers brought up large, shallow pewter bowls—called "basons"—and pewter dishes, bottles, and tankards or mugs.

When divers recovered the bowls, some were still sandwiched together with remnants of paper and straw packing material. These perplexed everyone. The bowls, or basons, were supposed to have been used as trade items in West Africa. Why, then, were they still being carried as cargo on the return trip to England?

Many thousands of glass beads for trading were also found. Beads were scattered from one end of the wreck site to the other. The same question was asked about them. Why were the beads being taken back to England?

In the journal of the slave ship *Albion Frigate*, David Moore found a possible answer. James Barbot, writing of the voyage to West Africa in 1699, noted that there was little demand among the native population for certain items. "The Blacks objected much against our wrought pewter

Dozens of shallow pewter bowls—called "basons"—were discovered at the wreck site.

Divers recovered many thousands of tiny glass beads (shown enlarged).

. . . our basons, tankards, yellow beads . . . green beads . . ." According to Barbot, the African traders were seeking large brass or copper rings, which were worn around the legs and arms. None of these were recovered from the *Henrietta Marie*.

The most unusual pewter discovery was a handsome two-gallon jug with a long, thin spout, a pair of curved handles, and a threaded pewter lid. When the jug was found, it was crushed almost flat and covered with a thick crust of marine growth. After it was washed off, the ends of spoons could be seen sticking out of the bottom. With careful pulling and prying, divers removed one after the other, a total of 72 in all. On the handle of each appears a portrait of King William III of England.

More than a dozen squatty, thin-necked pewter bottles were found, all about the same size and shape, able to hold a quart of liquid. Perhaps

Handsome pewter jug has curved handles, long spout, and threaded neck, but its use remains a mystery.

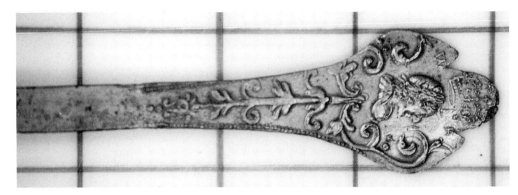

Pewter jug contained dozens of spoons like this one, each with an image of English King William III on the handle.

Pewter bottles, about one quart in size, may have been used for wine or liquor.

Some pewter plates were scarred with knife marks, indicating they were probably used as tableware.

Small decorative frames, made of lead, probably enclosed mirrors, which were popular as trade items. (Quarter is to show relative size.)

they were used for wine or liquor. "They're a great rarity," says David Moore. Pewter plates, each about nine inches in diameter, were scarred with knife marks, indicating they were used as tableware. The ship's initials, HM, appear on the reverse side of each plate.

Small lead frames were yet another trade item found at the *Henrietta Marie* sight. Slightly oval in shape, they resemble picture frames, but there was no photography in those days. Archaeologists believe the frames were used to enclose small mirrors which were highly prized by West African traders. The fragile mirrors shattered in the wreck.

Muskets, blunderbuss barrels, and cutlasses were found, and a number of items from the ship itself. One of these was the ship's compass; another was a bilge pump.

The compass was not found intact, but was recovered in two parts. The metal compass bowl in which the compass needle fit was crushed. Divers also found the pointer, or needle, itself. A bilge pump was used to empty the bilge water that accumulated in the bottom of a wooden sailing ship. "While it is not exactly unusual to find a bilge pump at a wreck site," said

Two blunderbuss barrels were found at site. A wooden stock and metal parts were added to one for display purposes.

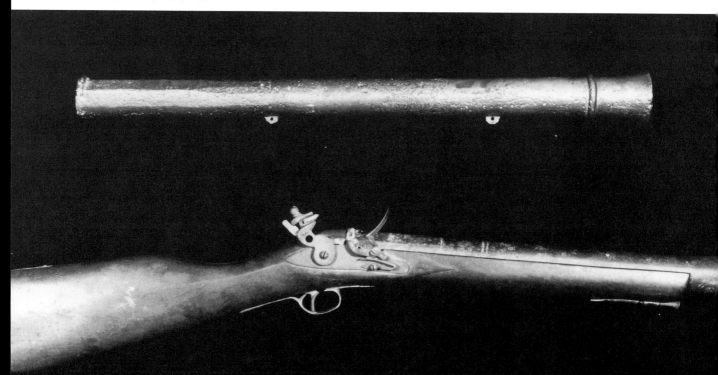

David Moore, "finding the upper part, where the handle is attached and the pumping action takes place, is indeed rare. I've never seen one."

Draft markers, used to indicate how deep the *Henrietta Marie* was immersed in the water at any given time, were found. Made of lead, the markers were cast as Roman numerals and divers brought up three—VII, VIII, and VIIII (7, 8, and 9).

An interesting discovery was 28 long, slim, flat, unfinished strips of iron, each about the size and shape of a foot-long ruler and weighing about two pounds. Except for some scarring and pitting that resulted from their long stay underwater, they looked pretty much as they had originally. One was stamped with the letter G within a circle; another was stamped FF. "No one knows what the markings mean," says Corey Malcom, "but we're working on it."

The strips of iron, called "voyage iron" by the slave traders, were trade items. At the time of the *Henrietta Marie*'s voyage, the continent of Africa was becoming more and more dependent on iron. African craftsmen are

Lead draft markers for the Henrietta Marie *were cast in Roman numerals.*

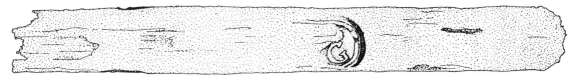

Foot-long iron strips were, like money, a medium of exchange.

likely to have heated the bars until they were red-hot, then pounded them into a wide array of tools or other implements to be used in agriculture, construction, or defense.

According to Corey Malcom, iron bars were brought to West Africa by the thousands and were looked upon, like money, as a medium of exchange. In 1693, Thomas Phillips, captain of the *Hannibal*, wrote that he was able to trade one iron bar for "1000 weight" of Malaga pepper, which was used for treating certain illnesses on slave ships. The captain of another slaver noted that brandy was valued at two iron bars per gallon.

Iron bars were also traded for human lives. James Barbot, of the *Albion Frigate*, wrote that after negotiations with a local king, he traded " . . . thirteen bars for males and nine bars and two brass rings for females . . ."

"It's horrifying," says Corey Malcom, "to think that these iron bars, which are among the cheapest of man-made items, could be exchanged for human lives."

"We have a very complete group of artifacts," says Madeleine Burnside, Executive Director of the Mel Fisher Maritime Heritage Society. "Each leg of the triangle trade is documented. The trade beads, pewter, and iron-bar currency represent the first stage of the voyage. The shackles are from the Middle Passage. From the third leg, we have the elephant tusks and pieces of dyewood, which were being brought back to England to be sold. And, of course, we have countless artifacts that represent the ship itself —the bell, hull and deck timbers, navigational instruments, cannons and cannonballs—just about everything. What we have tells the whole story."

8
Lessons of a Slave Ship

To marine archaeologists, the *Henrietta Marie* is an historical treasure, the source of an extraordinary collection of artifacts that provides a revealing look at the institution of slavery and its cruelties.

But to a group of a dozen black underwater divers who, on a sun-filled spring afternoon in 1993, gathered on the deck of a small boat anchored in the Gulf of Mexico at New Ground Reef, the *Henrietta Marie* represents much more. The divers, members of NABS, the National Association of Black Scuba Divers, were there to lower a marker to the site where the sand-covered timbers and other remnants of the *Henrietta Marie* still lie.

"There are lessons to be learned from people who survived slavery," says Oswald Sykes of Albany, New York. "There is so much to honor and respect with them."

The association of divers, which has some 1,500 members throughout the country, carried out the construction of the 2,700-pound memorial. Inside the concrete casting, a book of names was placed. They are the names of members of NABS and corporate contributors who helped finance the project. A bronze plaque is mounted to one side of the casting that reads:

HENRIETTA MARIE

IN MEMORY AND
RECOGNITION OF THE COURAGE,
PAIN AND SUFFERING OF
ENSLAVED AFRICAN PEOPLE.

"SPEAK HER NAME AND GENTLY TOUCH
THE SOULS OF OUR ANCESTORS."

Dedicated November 15, 1992

Most members of NABS first learned of the *Henrietta Marie* when David Moore and Corey Malcom, representing the Mel Fisher Maritime Heritage Society, brought some of the ship's artifacts to the 1991 annual meeting of NABS held in Fort Lauderdale, Florida. Oswald Sykes, who later was to head the NABS *Henrietta Marie* Project Committee, recalls that he and several other members cried when they first touched the shackles and other pieces of history.

"When you touch or hold an artifact, there is a bond or link between you and the last person to hold it, someone in antiquity," said Sykes. "Artifacts have power. Just being near them, seeing them, being in their presence, it has an electric effect; it has impact; it's emotional."

Sykes said that later he played back his tape of the television series "Roots," to see whether it had the same impact. The eight-episode TV series was based on the monumental book, *Roots, The Saga of an American Family*, published in 1976, in which author Alex Haley traced his bloodline back through several generations in the United States and several more in a village on the Gambia River in West Africa. "It wasn't the same thing," Sykes said. "When you hold the shackles, you feel a lot of pain. You realize the last people who saw those shackles were slaves.

"You cry a little. You can't look at them without feeling something."

NABS raised the money to finance the *Henrietta Marie* memorial project. The divers assembled in Key West in November, 1992, to set the monument in place, but stormy weather prevented them from doing so. They rescheduled the emplacement for May, 1993.

At the break of dawn on May 15, they met at a dock where a dive boat was waiting to take them to the wreck site, 35 miles due west across open water into the Gulf of Mexico. Reporters from newspapers in New York, Washington, Miami, and other cities also made the trip, as did two television crews. A separate boat was required for the monument.

The day was warm and clear, with a bright sun blazing; the sea was calm. During the 3½-hour trip to the site, the divers were quiet. Several of them spoke of their feelings with one another and the reporters.

"When people think of slavery, they think about people working on the plantations, they don't think about the abductions and the horrors," Hank Jennings told *New York Newsday*. "If you're a black American, you may have an ancestor who took that trip across the Atlantic, who knows? I can't imagine what it was like taking that journey into hell, but just knowing that our ancestors fought hard to survive under those conditions makes me a stronger and better person today."

When the work boat carrying the monument was spotted, the divers began to check their equipment and zip themselves into their lightweight wet suits. A second dive boat approached. It carried officials from the National Oceanographic and Atmospheric Administration (NOAA). NOAA had granted permission for emplacement of the monument, and they wanted to be sure that the coral reef and remains of the wreck were not going to be damaged in any way.

José Jones, one of the founders of NABS and Vice President at the time, and David Moore went into the water first to be certain the dive boat was at the wreck site. Although visibility below the surface was poor, they spotted metal rods and strands of polypropylene line that Moore had used in staking out the site boundaries years before. The monument, which was suspended a few feet below the surface by a pair of large plastic lift bags that floated in the water behind the stern of the work boat, was in a perfect position to be lowered.

At that point, the divers gathered in a circle on the deck of the dive boat and Oswald Sykes conducted a brief dedication ceremony. "We, the members of NABS, have this day come to this place to honor our African ancestors," he began. "Our visit here is testimony that we have not forgotten their suffering in the ocean crossings nor the great pool of talent they possessed. We are very much aware of their vast contribution to the development of the Western Hemisphere.

"If African Americans have survived the centuries since slavery began, it is in a large measure due to the courage, strength, and thoughtfulness of those people who were forced to travel the sea routes of death and suffering in vessels like the *Henrietta Marie*. They were determined to go on living.

"Even though no Africans were aboard the *Henrietta Marie* when she sank on the reef, we believe the spirits of a multitude of African people who died in transit are still with this sunken vessel. By remembering the slaves who sailed on this ship we can more fundamentally personalize the slave trade issues.

"We can call her by name, we know she existed," said Sykes, echoing

José Jones (left), then vice president of NABS, and David Moore plan their dive on boat trip to wreck site.

Memorial was suspended in the water from white plastic lift bags that trailed this work boat, then gently lowered to wreck site.

the words engraved on the plaque. "We can document her evil tasks, we can this day gently touch the souls of our ancestors."

Then, as the divers bowed their heads, Sykes quoted several lines from "Lift Ev'ry Voice and Sing," written by James Weldon Johnson in 1900 and often called the "African-American National Anthem."

We have come over a way that with tears have been watered,
We have come, treading our path through the blood of the slaughtered,
Out from the gloomy past,
Till now we stand at last
Where the white gleam of our bright star is cast.

When the ceremony ended, the divers entered the water in pairs. Two of them, José Jones and Ric Powell, then President of NABS, swam over to where the monument was suspended. They guided the concrete casting as it was slowly lowered through 30 or so feet of murky water to a sandy patch on the ocean floor.

Just before the monument came to rest, Jones turned the memorial so that the plaque faced east—toward Africa. "It was like we were sending a message back."

When the other divers descended to the bottom to examine the monument, they found a strong current running. They had to kick hard to be able to stay in one place long enough to read the inscription and run

Before lowering the memorial, NABS members held a dedication ceremony aboard the dive boat.

their fingers over the lettering on the bronze plaque. Several took photographs.

Some divers spoke of a spiritual connection with the *Henrietta Marie*. "It's an eerie connection," said Howard Moss. "There's a powerful presence down there."

Oswald Sykes rubbed the plaque and stared at the inscription. It was a deeply moving experience for him. When he returned to the dive boat, he spent a few moments alone, his face buried in his hands. "I could feel their souls," he said. "It was like I was touching them. I know they are there."

In the years ahead, the Mel Fisher Maritime Heritage Society plans to bring the story of the *Henrietta Marie* to as many people as possible. They have worked with scholars of African-American history in the development of a traveling exhibition of *Henrietta Marie* artifacts that is being made available to museums and other cultural institutions. The theme of the exhibition is the shared impact of the slave trade upon the economic, political, and cultural history of the people of West Africa, Europe, and the Americas. In addition to the artifacts, the exhibition includes maps, copies of crew members' wills, ships' logs, and models of the *Henrietta Marie* herself.

Russell Adams, chairman of the Afro-American History Department at Howard University in Washington, D.C., was one of the organizers of the exhibition. He points out the positive lessons to be learned from the slave trade and the *Henrietta Marie*. "The humanity of the folks was not destroyed by slavery. Their courage was tested, but not obliterated," he says.

America still lives with a legacy of sanctioned racism, inequality, segregation, and prejudice, says Adams. The battle goes on, he adds, but with hope.

"Just as slavery ended, racial practices can end. I grew up going to school in the back of the bus. Now my sister teaches in a desegregated school in Georgia.

"Change is possible."

Bibliography

Alderman, Clifford Lindsey. *The Story of New England's Triangular Trade*. New York: Macmillan, 1972.

———. *Wooden Ships and Iron Men*. New York: Walker, 1964.

Bean, Richard Nelson. *The British Trans-Atlantic Slave Trade, 1650–1775*. New York: Arno Press, 1975.

Dow, George Francis. *Slave Ships & Slaving*. Westport, Connecticut: Negro Universities Press, 1970 (Reprint of 1927 edition).

Equiano, Olaudah. *The Life of Olaudah Equiano, or Gustavus Vass, the African*. Boston: I. Knapp, 1837.

Howard, Thomas, ed. *Black Voyage: Eyewitness Accounts of the Atlantic Slave Trade*. Boston: Little, Brown, 1971.

Kay, F. George. *The Shameful Trade*. London: Muller, 1967.

Lyon, Eugene. *The Search for the Atocha*. Port Salerno, Florida: Florida Classics Library, 1979.

Mannix, Daniel P. and Malcolm Cowley. *Black Cargoes: A History of the Atlantic Slave Trade, 1518–1865*. New York: Viking Press, 1962.

Moore, David. *Anatomy of a 17th Century Slave Ship: Historical and Archaeological Investigations of "The Henrietta Marie 1699."* (A thesis presented to the faculty of the Department of History, East Carolina University, Greenville, North Carolina, 1989.)

Palmer, Colin A. *Human Cargoes: The British Slave Trade to Spanish America, 1700–1739*. Urbana, Illinois: University of Illinois Press, 1981.

Russell, Henry. *Human Cargoes: A Short History of the African Slave Trade*. New York: Longmans, Green, 1948.

Sullivan, George. *Treasure Hunt: The Sixteen-Year Search for the Lost Treasure Ship "Atocha."* Port Salerno, Florida: Florida Classics Library, 1993.

Index